Stop Pushing!! Pull!!

The Art of Winning with People

Shannon Marcum

Forward:

When I decided to write this book, my first thought was that I wanted to deliver something a busy leader could have time to read. Not sifting through endless pages of my personal experiences and resume to get to the messages that matter. I wanted this to be a quick read and easy to share with others, read and discussed. Get a highlighter and a pen and refer to this book as needed. The recurring statement in this book of; **You cannot give away something you do not own**, has served me well in all aspects of my life and I have seen vast improvements in others I have coached who have adopted and now live by this statement. The goal of this book is to help you generate more profit as a result of collective behaviors. Please make no mistake about profit being the goal but finding a path to sustainable growth starts with culture. Culture is the prequel to your brand story. Without a strong culture, you have no one to tell your brand story. Success is a group effort, and everyone is needed. Organic long-lasting success comes from an employee first culture. You cannot deliver your message to every customer. Your people will provide it and not just your front-line, EVERYONE.

Chapter 1. The Solution: Day 1

Chapter 2. The Money Cart is Killing Horse

Chapter 3. Get Out of Your Business

Chapter 4. Dumb Questions

Chapter 5. The Energy War

Chapter 6. Choking on Pizza

Chapter 7. Small Wins Large Returns

Chapter 8. Inspire, Energize and Expand

Chapter 9. Servant leadership

Chapter 10. Put me in coach

Chapter 11. You're ready for your close up

Chapter 12. Now give it all away!!

Chapter 1

The Solution: Day 1

Good morning, you are up early. You are reading and seemingly focused. You have pushed yourself to a place of success, and you are reaping the benefits of it. So why does it always feel like something is missing? The next step feels out of reach or like a void that keeps you from feeling that success is emulating all through your organization. As a leader, the frustration of others that surround you is hard to take at times. Building a strong culture requires thinking that is both uncomfortable and uncertain at first. The results are not immediate, and you will be met with resistance by those who this kind of change would make uncomfortable. By the unloyal tenured and those who are pay plan handcuffed and forced into silos. Changing culture is like battling monsters that you created. These monsters may have outgrown you and admitting this is a hard pill to swallow. But here we are, at the point, we must decide to take the monster on or be like the many examples whose companies fell or people who lost their position. These failures occurred because it is uncomfortable to change and met with resistance. First, we must identify the health of our culture. Not what the management perceives it to be but what is said about who you are at every level.

Let us first start by asking our employees. I recommend each employee take a completely anonymous culture and engagement survey administered by a third party. Several companies offer these kinds of engagement surveys. The employees will have to know that this is 100% anonymous or the results will be skewed and the sample worthless. These results will need to be collected, reviewed and analyzed. These results will give you a big-picture look at what is really going in on your culture. The natural reaction of a manager is to weaponize these results to correct peoples failures. We as leaders must learn to look at these results as a whole to understand behaviors that brought about the results. First looking at ourselves and we may create these behaviors. Remember loyal employees carry your message to the frontline. The danger is the when people filter that message to forward their agenda. These areas will become clear as you take pause with the results you have gathered and recognize patterns in behaviors.

We are witnessing a new era in business; customer service is no longer good enough. Hospitality is the new frontier. As I said you can only give away what you own and if your people are not excited about you, they will not get your customers excited about doing business with you. This goes way beyond perks and days off. Are you willing to empower them? Can you offer them a sense of safety that comes from confidence and purpose in a career that extends well beyond the tasks of just having a job? The careers and satisfaction of employees and customers almost mirror each other. If your people feel like what they have is just a job they will not be able to create career customers on your behalf. Your advocate career employees will develop lifelong relationships and generate career customers for you. But remember they cannot give away something they do not own. So, where does all of this come from? It starts with you.

Now the hard part begins, day one for you. Are you ready to take this journey to change and adapt against old lessons we have held onto so tight over the years? To believe in and live a new culture? To look at yourself and meet your values and brand statement in a place of action? If the answer is yes, let's begin.

On the first day of every year, I will often make some resolution about my health or financial goals. This year I decided I needed to make three lifestyle and mindset changes that would be tools I would use to work toward goals and not be discarded resolutions. This year I decided to be a better student, a better servant, and a better steward. Doing each of these every day has been a life changing experience for me and has transformed my relationships as a leader. In my journey as a leadership and culture coach, I find active listening to be my greatest acquired skill. Approach every conversation with the intent of being a student and learning something. If you want to be a teacher, coach or mentor, then you must first be a student. Learn something new every day. Not from just from books, videos, and social media but learn from those you intend to teach. Teach them to learn from others as well. From customers, other employees and even family. These skills are transferable to all aspects of life. Employees that are happier at home are happier at work. These skills a will improve all relationships in our life. The people

I coach that are getting it and living it has a vastly improved quality of life, but I notice they talk about their home life more as they learn to enhance all of their relationships.

Being a better servant allows for flipping the corporate pyramid. Managing people is a waste of time and energy. Demanding that others serve you and the customer at the same time is unrealistic and usually two different set of instructions. The employees are frustrated and give that away to the customers. Have you ever experience poor service at a restaurant and the waiter with a blushing face has to explain to you that the policy responsible for the poor experience is not their fault but management will not change it. Change requires leadership and part of that leadership is listening to and removing obstacles for the employee so that they can remove them for the customer. Doing this is a service to your employees. Don't let pride or confusion of perks cloud your judgment in being a servant leader.

Now for stewardship. The job of supervising or taking care of something, such as an organization or property. In this case, the resource is people. Everyone in your organization should be responsible to everyone else in it. After all this the culture you want to create for your customers. Then you should be living it when your customer is not around in preparation for their arrival.

Chapter 2

The Money Cart is Killing the Horse

So, you have a brilliant business model that supports an excellent product or service. On paper, the sky's the limit. You have run the numbers until you are blue in the face and everyone on your team could recite them in their sleep. Launch day is here, and the countdown has begun. You are fully staffed with brilliant people with the correct credentials. The processes are in place, and the product is flawless. The marketing team has conjured up a can't miss offer supported by some very shiny imagining. You have had several meetings and a few more meetings to clarify the previous sessions. Everyone knows what is expected of them. Hold on tight! We are about to get rich! 3…2…1… Flop!! How is this possible? You had everything in line. A boardroom full of brilliant minds, analytics, projections and cost analyzes. It was all right there in front of them on paper. You gave it to them on a silver platter. You pushed your team to the edge and made your expectations clear. Late nights and short lunches. You sacrificed personal time and family time as well. This is your baby, and you have given it all you have. Why was the market not inspired by this feat of greatness on your part?

There is a fact in any relationship, business or personal. **You cannot give away something you do not own**. We all want immediate gratification. In business, we want financial results. We want consumers to embrace our goods or services. For that to happen, the consumer must be inspired to connect with us on an emotional level. We are so caught up in the processes and numbers that we forget to inspire our people first or even worse we think they are already inspired. Are your employees emotionally connected to what you are doing? Do they understand why you are doing what you are doing? Are the people around you serving the greater good? Are you pushing them or pulling them along with you? Pulling is hard work. It is knowing and effectively communicating the true why of what you are doing. Then transferring the emotion of your why through your employees to your customers. Here are the scariest questions in business: Do you know or remember your why? What about the people under you? What about your front-line employees? How about the person that cleans the offices? If any of you say, money is your number one why most likely the previous scenario is familiar to you. Your cart is way out in front of your horse, and your culture is killing it. Of course, people work to fund their lifestyle but are they inspired to share your story. Are they a part of that story? What are they giving away to others? Are you sure? What is it that our favorite companies have in common? We say to ourselves, how did they get so big selling that! The secret is the "that" doesn't matter. The Why, the fact that they all know it and the transfer of energy to it is the reason they are so successful. All that preparation is the fundamental foundation of your offering and is a must, but it was lost to failure when taken to market. Every company has a what; few live the why. So, at this point, your mind may be racing around all the questions that were previously presented. More importantly, you have a few questions of your own. So……Start asking!

Most professionals worked their way up through the business that they are in. You may have been a great salesperson at one time and certainly have the right to speak to the subject of selling, but if that was 15 years ago, the game has changed significantly. Go to the frontline and ask your people what the obstacles are today and remove them. This will give you credibility by listening to them if you take action. They, in turn, will remove those obstacles for the customer and see it as a win for everyone. Their production will increase as well as their energy, and you will see the results. If you have a layer under you, they are responsible for coaching their people, and you should set the example by listening to them and serving their needs. They will pass it down if you inspire them. If you create this kind of buy-in at all levels of your company the main focus will be to service and increased profit will follow that organically. You will find that you are coaching less on stats and more on people and innovation.

Chapter 3

Get out of your business

Simple business formulas often get complicated by complex people. The reality is that most leaders are those complex people. We as a leader must possess the ability to simplify strategy and communicate it in the same language at every level of our business. For example, there are endless books on leadership strategy, and you could spend a lifetime researching them. Which as a servant and learning coach you should do but how do we gauge results? Take a breath and step back and boil that down to the lowest and most common denominator. The gauge for the effectiveness of a leader is simple, followers. That is the measurable result. This, of course, has various levels of success which by the way will be reflected in the body of work of your learning career. Most of the companies I speak to concerning culture have some varying degree of identity issues. They are confused about what business they are really in or who their direct customers are. If you own or manage a restaurant, you identify with being in the food industry and your customers are your patrons. Food is the what of your business and what I call inside the box processes. These should, in fact, be nearly flawless. They are the task and need to be managed. Your real business is your customers, and they are people. The business you are really in is the people business.

Often, we hear reference to outside the box thinking, but no one can define it. What is outside of this mythical box? Relationships and how we apply leadership to them is the real art of business. If you are the operator or owner of a company, it is safe to assume that you have people that you trust to manage these relationships on your behalf. You are paying these people to do so because you are only one person and could not possibly keep up the pace of necessary interactions it would take to sustain the volume of your business. Therefore, you or your most trusted staff hire and train people to interact with other people on your behalf to create commerce for your business. You are selling yourself, your beliefs and value system to these employees with the intended design of representing you. You are rarely talking to those patrons of your business to affect the result of creating commerce. Let's think about what business you are in and who is your direct customers. If you are in the people business and happen to sell or service whatever it is you have or do you need to realize that your direct customers are your employees. As in any sales job you need to bring to them the same passion, integrity, transparency, and values that you expect them to give to your customers. You cannot give away something that you do not own. Beware the pitfalls of lazy reasoning. I can't find good people. Our industry is harder than most. If these are your excuses you own them, if you buy into them don't be surprised when your employees pass them along through their actions to your customers. They can only give away what they have. Most of us are in a business that competes in a crowded market. We have products or services that are readily available through our competitors and at times at a lower cost. So, what is our only true equity resource? Our people! This is where the mythical outside the box exist and the space where consumers desire to pay for the experience. Think of it as a scale with one side the weight of experience and the other the weight is cost. When the experience side goes down the cost side goes up, and the customer begins to worry about price. When the experience side goes up cost is not so much of a factor, and we also see that true retention takes place in this space. It is the ease of doing business for our customers, the employee and patrons they are serving as well. Some companies operate in this space at such high levels that their customers rarely notice price increases. This is true retention, the ease of doing business on both sides. Not a geographical location or a coupon away from losing clients to competitors. Most leaders are stuck chasing task they believe to be their business. Doing this is the fast track to stalling growth. If you are indeed in the people business and set this example from the top down, it will reach your customers with ease.

Like any team, practice makes us perfect, and in business, the practice of building relationships starts internally and when it's game time the customers and employees feel they have won. In this space, your employees are empowered and will create. They will be less task driven and more purpose driven. This builds employee and customer retention. This is the space where true organic profit is born.

Chapter 4

Dumb Questions

The perception of most of the Managers and the perception of their employees are usually vastly different. That difference usually is unrecognized and therefore an assumption at best. We preach words like engagement and assume most everyone is engaged because we as leaders are. Let's play a grade school game, telephone. Take a group of ten employees you presume to be engaged. Bring them into a room to explain a new action item. Use something you are very excited about, and that is top of mind for you. Out of those ten do you think every person in the room 100% understands the item? Now let's say that you are a fantastic speaker and despite most studies seven out of ten of your people got it. Of the three who did not, two were embarrassed that they didn't get it and did not ask questions for fear of seeming below the intelligence bar for the room. So, they will ask someone to clear it up after the meeting. Who do you think they are most likely to ask? The smartest person the room who always gets it or someone else they feel safe with because they can read their frustration as well? Oh no! here comes meeting number two, which by the way you will not be attending. The break room meeting where the two of them guess at the meaning for an hour while they complain about the company's lack of communication and blame you for their confusion. The two are now further away from the objective and beginning the telephone game that we played in second grade. By the time the complaining and guessing make its way through all ten people and gets cleared up, morale has suffered and countless hours of productivity has been lost. The information is now differing significantly as filtered through the telephone game cycle. Now image its 50 employees or more. Image those Ten people are responsible for communicating this to 500 other employees. This, unfortunately, is common in workplace cultures.

People are starving for leadership to replace management. What they are looking for is very simple, to be emotionally connected to something greater than themselves. A leader to answer the questions, where are we going and how are we getting there? The remedy for this is at the top. You must foster a culture of learning. Stop making so many statements and ask more questions. Model a behavior where question asking is not only acceptable but expected. The only stupid question is the one not asked.

Have you been celebrating the cynical because they produce and appear witty? All the while suppressing less aggressive personality types who may outperform them in a better cultural climate. The cynics will discourage open discussions and cause you to lose credibility if you cater to them. We spend countless hours correcting bad behavior from talented pessimists. This time would be better served in the perpetuation of behaviors in those who live your story but perform averagely due to a lack of interest from their manager. The people at the assumed top you are so worried about as you ignore the middle which is the bulk of your people taking care of your business. Where do our employees learn their behaviors? Are they inspired and committed to your visions and values? What are you loading your employees with to deliver to your customers? Do your values and actions align? What behaviors are you modeling and is it regularly erased by inconsistencies on your part? Are we asking them to give away something they do not own or worse something that they perceive that you don't own yourself? These are hard questions, and usually, the answers are a result of decades of habits which can be changed.

Understanding what drives people is an art attached to science. It consists of the study of behavior and environmental influence. Like any art, practice is critical and starting on day one looks like a mountain that cannot be ascended. When we do begin the journey, we will transcend the glass ceiling of management to the endless sky of leadership. Listening with purpose is the most intelligent statement we can make as leaders. Active listening leads to our employees feeling confident to ask the questions that are really on their mind.

Chapter 5

The Energy War

Make no mistake; you are war. At war for the energy of your culture. It has many enemies, and you are paying most of them. Markets look to embrace companies that meet them where they want to be. Customers are looking for a connection beyond the transactional experience. There are failures in the best of transactions as they fall short of being interactions. On both the employee and customer sides of our business. When the transfer of emotional energy is absent, it forces the customer to make decisions based on logic and numbers. The real value of the experience of your offering has escaped, and the only value in your product or service is how much you are now willing to discount it. If your culture is void of positive energy, who will transfer it to your customers? If you do not have it, you cannot give it away.

You don't know what you don't know. We have heard this saying at some point in the business world. This statement is designed to ignite fear and should. If we have failed as leaders to transfer emotion and managed to rule and lord, how do we truly know the emotions that define our culture? What emotions if not those supported and transferred by our visions and values are being served up to our customers at every encounter? Encounters out of our site or worse supported by managers we created who are also outside of our purpose and brand statement. How then do we start to lead toward the known? Walk outside of your office right now and ask a few questions. Can the person directly under you with confidence define and articulate the purpose of your company? If you have a boss, could you with the same resolve, repeat it to them at any time without notice? The energy war rages on endlessly and needs constant, consistent and immediate correction and guidance. Leaders know and recognize who is providing energy to their culture and who is killing it. The best leaders take immediate action as to not sacrifice the many for the few. Acceptance of consistent undesirable behaviors from long-term employees is not a selling tool. They are selling your products or service but also selling out your credibility as a leader. The old "That's just how he/she is" rule for the problematic and tenured no longer has a place in the people business and the culture you are creating. The long-term effects of these behaviors are staggering. The new bright faces or the genuinely loyal in action will demote your credibility from leader to manager the first time you are seen tolerating or celebrating these behaviors. These bad actors are distracting from the war and keeping you in meaningless battles. This is a tremendous expense of time and resources and reflected in our bottom lines. When we lose focus on being accountable to our people and culture, all we have left is accountability to the task. Our discounted culture will only have that to give away, discounts. This is the hole that average companies are always digging out. A vicious cycle in the energy war. Today is doubtfully your first day, and these behaviors have been going on for some time. How do we change them in one day? You don't. Change is slow or short-lived it takes time and discipline. **You cannot give away something you don't own**. So, the secret to all this is starting with yourself first. You are reading and thinking about how to get better. Do your actions support your passions? The people around will see a change happening in you and crave to a part of it. This will get pushed down to your origination. It is very contagious when it is done right and consistent. People will desire to have the same the feelings and passion. Once this happens, you can pull people along. Remember change is a process, not an event.

Chapter 6

Choking on Pizza

Employee engagement is often mistaken for perks. We address despondency with trinkets and provide forums for our employees to migrate and discuss their lack of trust in our competency and credibility. If morale is at an all-time low and the actions that we are communicating as a company are uninspired, to say the least. Our people do not feel safe in their job and confidence is low. The manager with limited or no leadership skills decides the answer to this problem is a free lunch on a Wednesday. Is this an example of an offering of time and energy from the manager? No, yet the manager is expecting it in return for the gesture. Would you try these same tactics with a spouse or significant other? Honey, I know you have been unhappy for some time now. I brought you a pizza for lunch. It's on me. We are good now, Right? I think we can safely say pizza has never been the answer to mending any relationship. Yet we consistently skip the difficult task of leadership and shortcut it with meaningless gestures. Don't get me wrong if you are firing on all cylinders these get-togethers can create the desired effect but if used as a band-aid during times of at-risk culture they will surely backfire. Recognition can be a slippery slope if applied to merely evade the real problem for a while. Again, we are at a moment of transferring emotion. Why? is and should be the constant question. Why are we having free pizza Friday? Will we be using this time for something productive? What behaviors are you rewarding here? Chances are the ones involved have no idea. Worse they don't care and want a free lunch and think this is the most they can expect to gain from your relationship with them. I am not saying this is always a bad thing to do. If you gather your people with a purpose in mind and the culture is good, this is a great idea. Everyone desires to be a part of something greater than themselves. Rewards for employees should include empowerment, transparency, and confidence. Then celebrate reaching that point in your culture. The statement of people quit their boss, not their job is a hard truth. Trinket rewards also come to be expected as a form of compensation when morale is low, and these are the only events to look forward to happening. People who are empowered are confident and give that away to your customers who in turn are confident in your organization. When considering what to celebrate and tolerate also consider the environment in which you plan to do so. Great leaders have a purpose in every plan including free pizza.

Chapter 7

Small Wins Large Returns

Controlling expensive is a never-ending battle and a slippery slope culturally. The two opposable requirements for success are making what we have better and creating something new, and great leaders can do both. Removing obstacles for your employees gives way to the path of improvement of the current business model and space for clarity to create. Your environment should be inclusive of opening innovation. Employees at every level are being heard and could design thought both inside and outside of their role. They should also have a format to share these ideas. Suggestion sites or open forum meetings for input should be encouraged, and you should require your leadership make sure they are happening. Never discount an entry-level employee's idea on upper-level solutions. Remember your frontline is your bottom line. If you have been promoted out a job for years now, you will certainly welcome input from the person currently doing that job in an environment you did not experience. Being heard is a win and fosters confidence and provides a sense of inclusion. You must become a professional listener. Listen with purpose and not waiting to talk. This does not require you to become a "yes" leader and try to implement everything you hear. Quite the opposite, great leaders know how to say no. Not in a dismissive manner but absorb and recognize the validity and the reason you are receiving this information. When you do use the information to exact change, it will be recognized by your employees that their input counts toward removing obstacles and promoting change. This empowers your greatest asset, your people. This creates and builds confidence. In this environment, mistakes become lessons and can be shared and accounted for without fear. Image your culture firing on all cylinders and an employee teaching from a mistake they made instead of scrambling to cover it up. Remember you cannot give away something you do not own. If you want the market to embrace you with confidence, embrace your employees with it first. Set the stage for what people will see when they encounter your organization. If you want to be easy to be business with, make it easy for your employees to do that business. Are your leadership techniques designed to reduce the probability of errors and defects to occur by the removal of obstacles of doing business or are you just making policy, process, and rules to govern people? Are you holding on to years old policies that were made to police staff they may not even be with you anymore? For example,

An employee was stealing office supplies five years ago. So, the supplies had to lock away, and a rigorous process implemented to get those supplies. The employee may have stolen upwards of $100 in supplies and has been gone for three years. Is it still necessary to have this policy that cost many production hours and moral to protect $100 from a person that no longer works with you? This is a display of not trusting people who have great character and punishing them for the character of someone that you hired that is no longer here. It's easy to forget these policies are in place and have become the norm. The complaint of an employee who is saying "I have to jump through hoops to get copy paper for the copier at this place" is a criticism that should not be taken lightly. This will be perceived as a trust and character issue. If you are having these kinds of petty problems such as small theft, it's time make some hard decisions about the character of a few suffocating your moral. Even if it is your top performers, you cannot let these people's actions speak for your brand. No amount of advertising will sway the public opinion your culture creates. What are you saying as an organization to your customers? Are we in the mode of defending what we have or growing to get more?

Chapter 8

Inspire, Energize and Expand

Now that you know you are fighting the energy war it is time to plant that flag firmly in the minds and hearts of those you wish to rally. Use this energy as fuel every day. What is next in this journey? It is time to inspire. What do people see you do? Get out there and connect with the energy of your people. Ask them how they are doing with genuine intent and purposeful listening. They will return that favor as they see you give it away to them and others. Talk to them and let them know what you are working on currently. Transparency is inclusion, and that makes people want more. More of you and what you are doing. Talk about what books you are reading, videos you have watched and anything that you are doing to improve yourself. Ask them about themselves and answer when they ask about you. You will see it is contagious and people want to be in your circle and on your team. The day to day small task and opportunities that used to weigh you down are now being handled without you. Freeing up your time to work on big-picture projects. This will allow you to create and innovate those amazing ideas your empowered workforce has been bringing to you. Most likely improving your workplace culture and improving your employee's quality of life and in turn improving yours. There is no neutral in business, and your company is spiraling up or down, always. All the great leaders that inspire you to understand this and work it every day. They move their purpose statement through every action and encounter of every employee, every time. They may not have every answer, but they know for sure that one of their people do and they trust and empower that person. Things keep moving. Obstacles get removed, and the customer feels that. If you haven't had the courage or conviction to remove the people killing your culture, now is the time to act. If you have the right people, let them do the right things. They will grow your business for you with the guidance of your leadership. Take action and handle personnel opportunities upstream. This will energize your genuinely loyal employees by showing them that you have their best interest in mind and truly value the culture. Now that you are inspiring you people, the energy is high, and you people are growing your business who knows what will happen. Remember when Amazon only sold books, Netflix mailed out DVD's and Apple just sold computers. These changes would have been impossible without a healthy culture. These companies inspired and energized their people. People are the only difference in a crowded market and ideas are old soon after they are invented. How strong is the culture you are betting the future of your company? Leaders are only defined by one factor. Followers.

Chapter 9

Servant Leadership

Lording over people and servicing old ideas have become the newest extinct animal in the business world. Like everything that grows it also evolves, and the climate of business has vastly changed in recent years. The world is shrinking as technology brings us closer than ever before. It has become very easy to find the opinions of others, and those opinions are valued be they right or wrong. The perception is more than ever reality and now being served like it is on tap. Your employee and your customer engagement and satisfaction live on a mirrored plain. If you survey both with similar questions about your company, you would see how close the answers are. You cannot give away what you do not own. You should be surveying both regularly. You employees with 100% anonymity so you can get the real data about the culture of your company. I would imagine if you asked them these three questions the result would be surprising. 1. I trust my manager. 2. I trust my fellow employees and 3. My opinion matters at this company. If the results come back low, It's time to humble up and get to work. This work requires service. You are responsible for the people responsible for the work. This is your job as a leader and the way to gauge if your people are following.

If they are, all the spreadsheets will indicate this by showing sustainable and organic growth. Let think back to your purpose statement. Who should be the first person living by this statement? You cannot give away something you do not own. You are responsible for these people. If they are good employees and advocates for your company, you are accountable for their quality of life at work, which should be carrying over to their home life. If they are not, you are responsible for letting them go. Don't allow them to fail in a job that doesn't move their quality of life forward. This responsibility should resonate throughout your origination. Who is responsible for the culture? Everyone but the heavy lifting starts at the top. Flip the pyramid. If you have 50 employees or 50,000, you should be in constant service to them through the values and purpose of your organization. A servant leader gives all he has away and gets more in return. Then starts over every day. Yes, this is how to get more. By providing more of yourself away. You time and energy that got you where you are. Your position is not a finish line or an end to a goal. It is a starting line and a time to be more humble and learn more than ever. Your frontline is your bottom line and if you are not in service to them who is? If they feel no one is, how are making your clients feel? Great leaders are not in fear of words like humility and service. That fear comes from the unknown. The fear of the realization that your people will know you don't have it and can not give it away or the perception of that you don't give it away because you don't know what it is. Be a servant, look back on the great leaders of our history and recount what they did in service of others.

Chapter 10

Put Me in Coach

Let us now talk about the empowerment of these great employees. For years we have felt the weight of doing it all. Maybe we were thought by a mentor that doing it all is the kind of focus that gets you ahead. A never-ending drive of long hours and face-time management. Saying things like I am the hardest worker here. I put in 80 hours this week, and I am the first one in and the last one out. Even at the sacrifice of missing family events and dinners, doing homework with your children or time with your significant other. Without this balance in life and the stress of the lack of that balance, what are you giving away to your people? You know you cannot fake a mood it's just science. Your brain is either producing happy chemicals like dopamine and oxytocin or sad ones like high levels of cortisol or low levels of serotonin. I am by no means any type of doctor, but I am a student of behavior and the effects of those behaviors on those around us. We refer to this as a "gut" feeling because we have the ability to read these chemical reactions in others instead we know we can or not. We also infer emotional states from facial expressions. This was a long way to get to a short fact. You can't fake it. What insurances can we put into place in a busy world that we don't fall into these emotional trappings? After all, we do have an amazing resource at hand, our people. How do we affect the balances of you and those around you? Empower them to do what you hired them to do. If they are indeed the right people and their values align with yours, why do we feel the need to micro-manage them? If we are putting our hands on everything, they do how will they learn from mistakes you never let them make. The dangerous side of this is that we may suppress innovations that we could not have formulated on our own. This impedes progress at every turn. If they are consistently looking over their shoulder for our approval, there will be no room for original thought. So, let them go!

Doing this will give you a real assessment of the talents you have and not a watered-down version of yours. This will also allow you to work on the big picture projects and your life balance. Quality work hours versus quantity work hours chasing others task. Make no mistake the mood at the top is the current mood of the entire company. If you don't believe that show them the slightest hint of fear and wait for the rumors to come back to you. They will turn your concern of a slight rise in the cost of goods into massive layoffs within hours. The upside to this is that if we empower people and keep our balances in place even in times of downturn, we can endure and make our company more recession proof with an empowered workforce that may not even notice industry trends and powers through them. Zappos, who has a very inspired people driven leader in Tony Hsieh and a healthy culture experienced a significant increase in the tumultuous market of 2008. Selling mainly shoes. Stop being a boss and start being a coach.

Chapter 11

I am Ready for My Close Up

As we transform from managers into servant leaders, transparency becomes more important than ever. Have you ever had the displeasure of working for someone with low visibility? Yes, all professionals are busy, and that business requires times behind closed doors. What I am referring to is the truly invisible. The ones who have made considerable effort to be out of sight. I have made some references to fear throughout this book and the effects of it. The perception and the reality of fearful leadership are they may be asked the one question they cannot answer, why? Even worse the only conclusion they can present is to increase profit which is a result of actions and not in and of itself an action. Which by the way, even your most entry-level employees can smell this fear when given this answer. It represents a finishing point and a person who feels they too are at a finishing point. This finality is not in line with a learning culture with the goals of new beginnings and future success. So, what is a visible leader? First, let's revisit fear and the cause of it in leadership. The most glaring quality of visible leaders is confidence. Not the ugly and dreadfully behavior of someone who is desperate to cover up flaws by peacocking and posturing but genuine confidence. The kind that comes from the ability to show everyone where we are going and how we are getting there. That your passions are supported by your actions and in line with your purpose statement. The kind which they identify with and support because their opinions are represented in that statement. They are craving more of you. They want to be more like the company culture you have all created together. They want to read what you are reading because you are talking about it. They want to work on themselves to improve their surroundings. This is the fabric of a learning and teaching culture that produces impressive profit as a result. It is organic and not a forced failure through panic. You may not be able to see every employee on a regular basis if your company is large, but they will see you. What is their take away for what they see? Even employees in other locations get an impression of you from others. You can't give away what you do not own. When you are being discussed among your employees what is being given away?

Chapter 12

Now Give It All Away

The culture and moral are now at an all-time high. Customers are feeling it and discounts has been replaced by experience. Those numbers you have been chasing for years are happening organically. The inside the box processes are perfect, and the outside the box experiences have graduated from excellent customer service to exceptional hospitality. You have moved your employees and customers from transactions to interactions. True retention on both sides is no longer at risk to a coupon or a slight pay increase at your competitors. Your culture is now a living ball of energy and has become part of the fabric and a way of life at your company. Everyone wants to do business with you, and everyone wants to work with you. So, what now? Obtaining something difficult requires a change in mindset. A new way of thinking is a tremendous undertaking. The time and energy it takes to get there are strenuous and challenging. So, is this the finish line? What companies fail to communicate to their people is that there is no finish line. Your organization is now one of learning and development. What is hard to gain is easy to lose, unfortunately. Like most sports teams that win a world or national championship, the real challenge is repeating.

Coaching and teaching are now more critical than ever as you transition from employing people at a job to developing people in their career. This ensures long-term growth beyond your years at the company. It is time to play the long game now with your new culture. Do all of your key positions have a number two person in place ready to step up in growth cycle? Are your managers not willing to give away what they have in fear of someone taking what they have got? Part of the humility of a great leader is the ability to give it all away knowing you will get more in return than you ever had. You should be in a state of what I call a plug and play culture. It is no longer defined by the individual people. The culture is defining the organization by having the right group of people in it. Based on the transfer of emotion through your vision, values, and purpose, your brand is preceded by your culture. New people will come on, and seasoned employees may leave or retire. The in the box processes such as hiring and onboarding should now be such that you have the ability to pull someone out and put someone in seamlessly. Not to hire robots by any means because new perspective is a gift but it should be used within the expectations of your culture. Hire culture and train talent. This will increase loyalty and allow you to promote from within those who already understand your culture and share your vision.

Image the luxury of not having to hire outsiders to run your company with lessons from someone else's culture. Which if they left where they were the culture was most likely not good. Now there is value everywhere you look and people who cannot wait to overpay for amazing service or product. Culture is also the ultimate succession plan. If you want more, learn more, get humble, serve and give it all away.

www.ingramcontent.com/pod-product-compliance
Lightning Source LLC
Chambersburg PA
CBHW070125230526
45472CB00004B/1423